Caleb and His Human

Author: Tasha Kanice Haywood

Illustrator: Julie Gullman

ISBN: 9781701205109

DEDICATION

This book is dedicated to my Granny Pearline. She led me to read many children's books as a child, and that is what inspired me to write this one. Thank you, Granny!

ACKNOWLEDGMENTS

I thank God for giving me the strength and the patience to write this book. I love that You led me to Caleb. When You whispered "That's him" I knew Caleb was just for me. Thank You!

Caleb you are my sweetie. My special and unique fur baby! My one and only hun bun! If it wasn't for you and all of the funny things you do this wouldn't be possible.

I thank my church family Pastor Dr. Timothy Hawkins, Sister Rachel Hawkins, and Sister Barika Culberson for leading the way for me write and self-publish. Sister Barika, thank you for extending all of your publishing resources to me get this done!

To my illustrator, Julie Gullman, GIRLLL, you knocked it out the park (no pun intended). LOL! You have a gift for drawing and with this book we will let the world know.

I have to thank all who edited this book. Sister Silva, your sharp eye to detail is amazing! Thank you for holding me accountable and checking to make sure I got this done.

Lorraine, thank you for all your suggestions and corrections at the midnight hour! No words can explain the thoughtfulness you showed during this process. I appreciate you taking my "About the Author" picture, and I appreciate your suggestions on how to make my picture POP!

Krista, thank you for doing the final edit. I appreciate all of your suggestions and corrections.

ACKNOWLEDGMENTS

Lastly, Chip Dunlap, thank you for reviewing this, as well. Your kind words inspired me to go on.

To my BFF Tiffany, thank you for listening to me and encouraging me to keep on and checking in with me to see when things were finished.

To my mother and father, thank you for all of your love and support, and for listening to all of my re-reads.

To my Dream Coach John Erik and Adventure Social, thank you for showing me how to take my dream of writing a children's book and effectively push forward to make it a reality.

To the children, parents, grandparents or whomever purchases this book, thank you for investing and believing in me. This project is made just for you! It's a piece of me that shows you that dreams really do come true. Enjoy!

Lastly, for those who are creatives and are striving to reach their goals, I want this book to inspire you to keep working at what you do. You may have to encourage yourself often but never give up! Philippians 4:12

I have a human who takes care of me.

Hi, my name is Caleb. I have a human. Her name is Tasha. I adore her.

She rubs my belly, and she feeds me yummy food.

I'm her best friend and she is mine.

One of our pastimes is walking at the park.

Her keys jingle when it's time to go.

She places me in the backseat. I'm always so excited! I can't keep still, so I jump from the back to the front, wagging my tail.

She tells me, "Caleb, calm down. Sit still." I try my best, but I still stick my head out the window.

I like to look at the park from the car window and smell the fresh
air. I want to walk right now, so I begin to bark and whine.

I know when we are close to our walk when Tasha clips on my leash on my harness.

This park is so GUUD! It's big, clean, and smells amazing!

I like to walk slow so I can smell every flower. Tasha walks fast and tells me, "Come on Caleb, let's walk!"

But today, I don't listen. I start to walk slower as she pulls me to walk faster.

I pull back and squeeze my shoulders together, and I slip out of my harness and I RUN.

She chases after me. The sun and the cool breeze feel good on my fur.

Tasha catches up to me and says, "Caleb, bad dog!
This park wants all dogs on a leash for safety reasons, and
we have to do what's right!"

I listen and I let her put the leash and harness back on me again.

We begin to walk together.

Then I hear some noises in the bushes and a big dog comes towards me.

I get scared because he's big and scary.

Tasha grabs me up quickly. The dog tries to bite at me,
but I feel safe in Tasha's arms.

Tasha tells the dog, "Go home! Get out of here!" The big dog gets
scared of her and runs away.

She places me back on the ground so we can walk together again.
It's really better to listen to my human. She knows best. I'm so
glad Tasha takes good care of me.

THE END.

Well maybe not....

Made in the USA
Las Vegas, NV
08 January 2022

40817679R00017